CONTINENTS

Antarctica

Leila Merrell Foster

Heinemann
LIBRARY

www.heinemann.co.uk/library
Visit our website to find out more information about Heinemann Library books.

To order:
☎ Phone 44 (0) 1865 888066
   Send a fax to 44 (0) 1865 314091
   Visit the Heinemann Bookshop at www.heinemann.co.uk/library to browse our
   catalogue and order online.

First published in Great Britain by Heinemann Library, Halley Court, Jordan Hill, Oxford OX2 8EJ, part of Harcourt Education. Heinemann is a registered trademark of Harcourt Education Ltd.

Editorial: Kathy Peltan, Clare Lewis, and Katie Shepherd
Design: Joanna Hinton-Malivoire and Q2A Creative
Picture research: Erica Newbery
Production: Helen McCreath

Origination: Modern Age Repro House Ltd.
Printed and bound in China by South China Printing Co. Ltd.

13-digit ISBN 978-0-431-15806-8 (hardback)
10 09 08 07 06
10 9 8 7 6 5 4 3 2 1

13-digit ISBN 978-0-431-09894-4 (paperback)
11 10 09 08
10 9 8 7 6 5 4 3 2

British Library Cataloguing in Publication Data
Foster, Leila Merrell
Antarctica. – 2nd ed. – (Continents)
919.8'9
A full catalogue record for this book is available from the British Library.

Acknowledgements
The publishers would like to thank the following for permission to reproduce photographs: Tony Stone/Ben Osborne p. **5**; Earth Scenes/David C. Fritts p. **6**; Tony Stone/Kim Heacox p. **7**; Peter Arnold/Gordon Wiltsie pp. **8**, **13**; Getty Images/National Geographic/Ralph Lee Hopkins p. **10**; Tony Stone/Kim Westerskov pp. **11**, **17**, **28**; Photo Edit/Anna Zuckermann p. **15**; Photo Edit/Jack S. Grove p. **16**; Bruce Coleman/Fritz Polking, Inc. p. **20**; Animals Animals/Johnny Johnson p. **21**; Earth Scenes/Stefano Nicolini p. **22**; Earth Scenes/Patti Murray p. **23**; Corbis/Bettmann Archive p. **24**; The Granger Collection p. **25**; Peter Arnold/Bruno P. Zehnder p. **27**; Earth Scenes/B. Herrod p. **29**.

Cover photograph of Antarctica, reproduced with permission of Science Photo Library/ Tom Van Sant, Geosphere Project/ Planetary Visions

The publishers would like to thank Kathy Peltan, Keith Lye, and Nancy Harris for their assistance in the preparation of this book.

Every effort has been made to contact copyright holders of any material reproduced in this book. Any omissions will be rectified in subsequent printings if notice is given to the publishers.

Some words are shown in bold, **like this**. You can find out what they mean by looking in the glossary.

Contents

Where is Antarctica?

A continent is a very large area of land. There are seven continents in the world. Antarctica is further south than any other continent. This makes it very cold there.

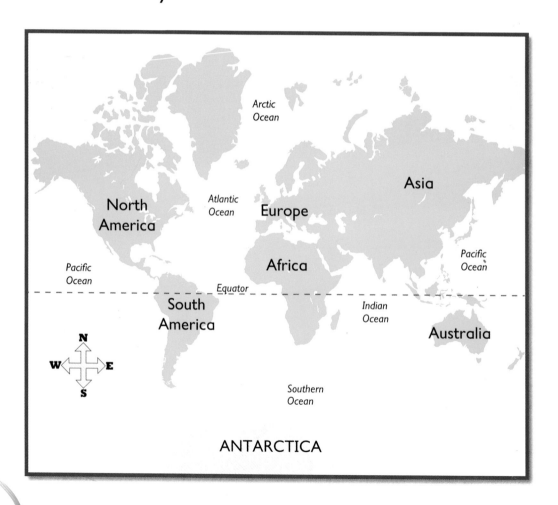

The world's lowest temperature was recorded in Antarctica. It was -89.2°C (-128.6°F).

▲ Snow-covered mountains in Antarctica

The **South Pole** is at the centre of Antarctica. Close to the South Pole, the sun sets only once a year. It is dark for six months in winter and light for six months in summer.

Ice sheet

It is so cold in Antarctica that the snow does not **melt**. The snow builds up into layers of ice. The ice covers nearly all of the land. This is known as the Atlantic **ice sheet**.

▲ *Mountains buried under ice*

The Antarctic ice sheet holds more than two thirds of all the fresh water in the world.

▲ **Iceberg** *close to the ice*

The Antarctic ice sheet is very thick. If it ever melted, the level of all of the seas in the world would rise by 60 metres (almost 200 feet). All the towns and cities along the coasts would disappear underwater.

South Pole

On the map there is a circle called the Antarctic Circle. It is an imaginary line that goes around the continent of Antarctica. Almost all of Antarctica is inside the Antarctic Circle.

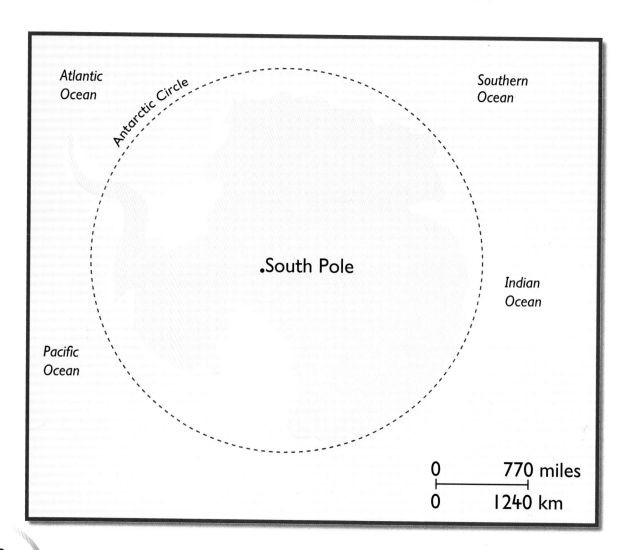

Atlantic Ocean

Southern Ocean

Antarctic Circle

.South Pole

Indian Ocean

Pacific Ocean

| 0 | 770 miles |
| 0 | 1240 km |

▲ Pole marking the South Pole

The **North Pole** and the **South Pole** are the furthest places from the **Equator**. The Equator is an imaginary line around the centre of the earth. The North Pole is in the Arctic. The South Pole is in Antarctica.

Weather

In summer, some of the ice at the edge of the **ice sheet melts**. In winter, the sea at the edge freezes again. This frozen seawater is called pack ice.

▲ *Penguins on an iceberg*

Antarctica is the coldest and windiest place on Earth.

▲ *Icy desert in central Antarctica*

In the centre of Antarctica there is an icy **desert**. Very little snow falls there, but sometimes there are **blizzards** that last for days. Human skin can freeze in 60 seconds. Even in summer, the temperature hardly ever gets above **freezing point**.

Mountains

The Transantarctic Mountains run right across Antarctica. They divide the continent into two areas. The areas are called Greater Antarctica and Lesser Antarctica. Greater Antarctica is a massive **dome** of ice.

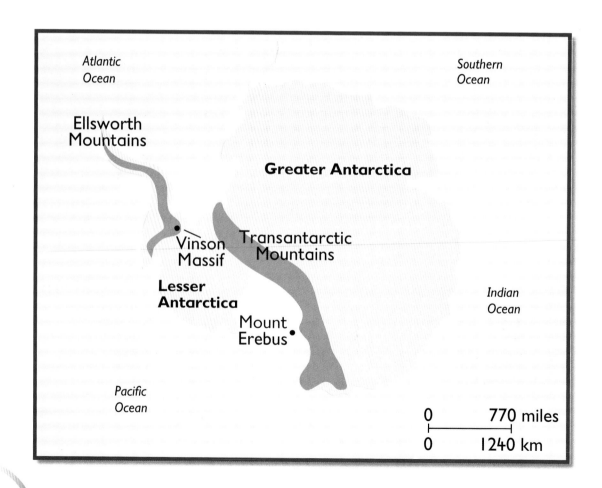

The Vinson Massif is the highest point in Antarctica.

▲ *The Vinson Massif in the Ellsworth Mountains*

The Vinson **Massif** is in the Ellsworth Mountains in western Antarctica. Mount Erebus is an **active volcano**. Mount Erebus often **erupts**, and throws out rocks.

Ice

Huge shelves of ice hang over the sea around the edges of Antarctica. They are called ice shelves. Some of these ice shelves are huge. When chunks of ice break away in the summer months, they form **icebergs**.

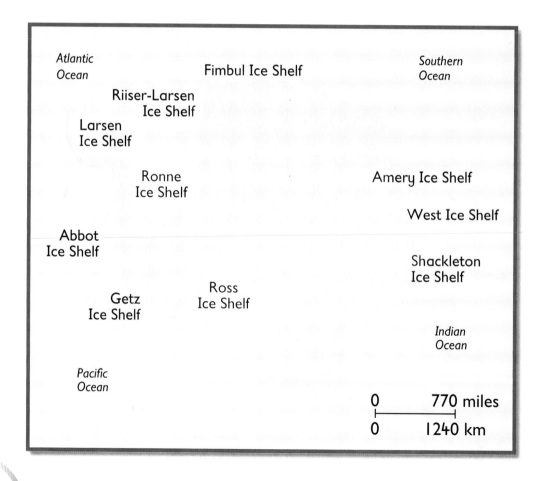

Atlantic Ocean

Fimbul Ice Shelf

Southern Ocean

Riiser-Larsen Ice Shelf

Larsen Ice Shelf

Ronne Ice Shelf

Amery Ice Shelf

West Ice Shelf

Abbot Ice Shelf

Shackleton Ice Shelf

Getz Ice Shelf

Ross Ice Shelf

Indian Ocean

Pacific Ocean

0	770 miles
0	1240 km

Most of an iceberg is hidden below the water.

▲ *Icebergs drift in the ocean*

Strong **currents** carry the icebergs out to sea. Icebergs are very dangerous for ships. This is because they are much larger than they seem. It can take many years for icebergs to **melt** and crack apart.

Glaciers

The continent of Antarctica is shaped like a **dome**. Ice is formed in the high centre of Antarctica. Then the ice slowly slides down the slopes of the dome to the edge of Antarctica. These slow rivers of ice are called **glaciers**.

▲ *Glacier on the Antarctic coast*

The Lambert Glacier is the world's largest glacier.

▲ Ice cliff at the edge of a glacier

The ice at the bottom of the glacier gets squashed by the ice above. Then the whole glacier slowly slides forwards. Glaciers often look like huge cliffs of ice.

Antarctica is surrounded by the icy cold Southern Ocean. There are also smaller seas closer to the land. The Southern Ocean stops the warmer water in other oceans from reaching the ice, so the ice does not **melt**.

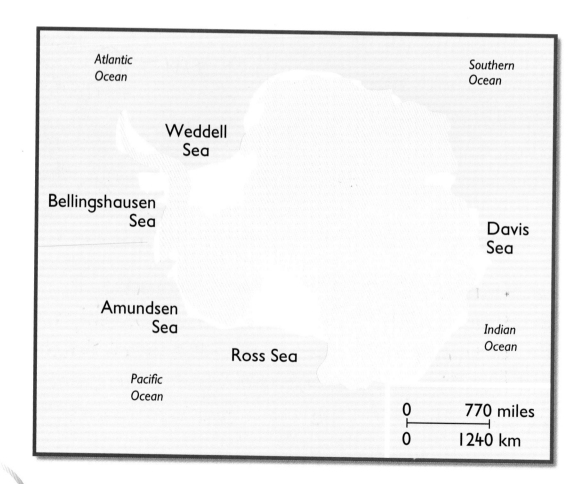

Atlantic
Ocean

Southern
Ocean

Weddell
Sea

Bellingshausen
Sea

Davis
Sea

Amundsen
Sea

Indian
Ocean

Ross Sea

Pacific
Ocean

0   770 miles

0   1240 km

▲ *Stormy weather in the Southern Ocean*

The Southern Ocean has strong **currents**. It has strong winds and huge waves. Most ships that go to Antarctica leave from the tip of South America. The journey takes three days in calm weather. When it is stormy it can take weeks.

Animals

Most birds that visit Antarctica fly north for the winter. But penguins stay in Antarctica all year round. Penguins have a thick layer of fat, and soft feathers to keep them warm. They are excellent swimmers. They catch fish from the sea.

▲ *Emperor penguins and their babies*

▲ *An elephant seal's nose looks like an elephant's trunk*

There are also seals and whales. The seals spend most of their time hunting for fish in the icy seas. People used to hunt the whales and seals that live in Antarctica. Now there are laws to protect them.

Plants

Lichen is the most common plant in Antarctica. It grows on rocks. It needs very little water to survive. Some types of moss also grow in Antarctica. Moss and lichen grow very slowly.

Some of the moss and lichen plants in Antarctica are more than 1,000 years old.

▲ *Lichen growing on rocks*

Tussock grass is the only grass that grows in Antarctica.

▲ *Tussock grass in northern Antarctica*

No trees grow in Antarctica. Only two types of flowering plant have ever been found there. Tussock grass is a type of grass that is found in the warmest parts of the continent. It has very strong roots to stop it being blown away.

Explorers

Early explorers sailed to Antarctica in wooden ships. But the sea ice trapped their boats. A British explorer called Ernest Shackleton escaped from his ship in a lifeboat. Some of his crew drifted for five months before they reached land.

▲ *Ernest Shakleton's ship trapped in ice*

Roald Amundsen used sleds pulled by dogs to carry his things.

▲ *The Norwegian explorer, Roald Amundsen*

Roald Amundsen was the first person to reach the **South Pole**. He reached it in 1911. A British explorer, Robert Scott, reached the South Pole in 1912. He used ponies to pull his sled. Sadly, he died on the journey home.

Research stations

Antarctica is the only continent with no countries. Many countries send scientists there to work in **research stations**. These scientists do **experiments** on the ice. The map shows some of the main stations in Antarctica and the countries they belong to.

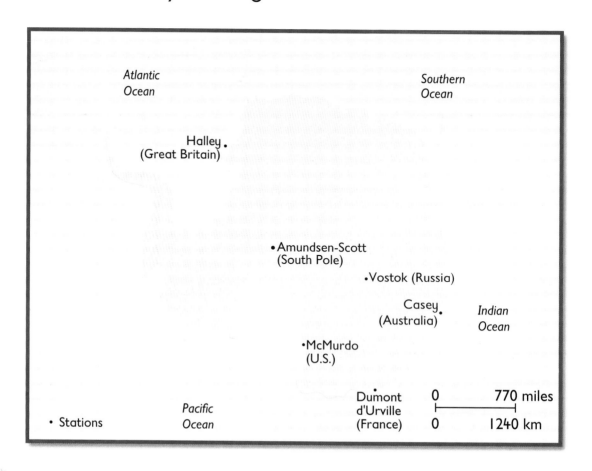

Atlantic Ocean

Southern Ocean

Halley (Great Britain)

•Amundsen-Scott (South Pole)

•Vostok (Russia)

Casey (Australia)

Indian Ocean

•McMurdo (U.S.)

Pacific Ocean

Dumont d'Urville (France)

• Stations

0   770 miles
0   1240 km

▲ *McMurdo research station in Antarctica*

In 1959, 12 countries agreed to keep
Antarctica free for peaceful research.
Mining is not allowed there. During
the summer, small groups of tourists visit
Antarctica. They must not leave any rubbish.

Science

Scientists study the weather in Antarctica. This helps them understand the weather all over the world. They measure how much ice **melts** in summer. They have discovered that more ice melts each year. This means the world's weather is getting warmer.

▲ *Scientists using a weather balloon to test gases in the air*

▲ Setting up equipment on the ice

Some scientists drill into the ice to find out what the weather was like hundreds of years ago. Other scientists in Antarctica study animals and plants, or use powerful telescopes to look at the stars.

Fast facts

Antarctica's highest mountains

Name of mountain	Height in metres	Height in feet
Vinson Massif	4,897	16,077
Mount Tyree	4,852	15,918
Mount Kirkpatrick	4,528	14,855
Mount Markham	4,350	14,271
Mount Erebus	3,794	12,448

Antarctica's record breakers

The coldest temperature ever recorded was at Vostock Research Station, Antarctica, in 1983. It was -89.2 °C (-128.6 °F).

No rain falls on the land in Antarctica. It only rains around the edge of the coast.

Winds in the Southern Ocean around Antarctica can reach speeds of 300 kilometres (about 185 miles) an hour.

At its thickest point, the ice covering Antarctica is almost 5 kilometres (about 16,000 feet) deep. Most of the ice in Antarctica is about 2 kilometres (6500 feet) deep.

Antarctica contains two thirds of the world's fresh water in the form of ice.

The biggest **iceberg** ever seen was larger than Belgium. It covered about 30,000 square kilometres (around 11,600 square miles).

The Lambert Glacier is more than 400 kilometres (250 miles) long and 80 kilometres (50 miles) wide.

Scientists have found fossils in Antarctica. This means that the continent was once warm, and that trees and other plants lived there.

Glossary

active volcano hole in the earth from which hot, melted rock is thrown out

blizzard snowstorm in which surface snow is picked up by strong winds

current movement of water

desert area with very little rain

dome rounded shape, like half a ball

Equator imaginary circle around the exact middle of Earth

erupt to throw out rocks and hot ash

experiment test to show or prove something

freezing point 0°C (32 °F) - the temperature at which water freezes

glacier very large mass of slow-moving ice and snow

iceberg large piece of ice that floats in the sea

ice sheet very thick layer of ice that covers a large area of land

massif mountainous area with lots of peaks

melt become liquid through heat

mining digging up things from under the Earth's surface

North Pole most northern spot on Earth

research station place where scientists work to find out new things

South Pole most southern spot on Earth

Mor books to read

Watching Penguins in Antarctica, Louise and Richard Spilsbury
(Heinemann Library, 2006)

My World of Geography: Oceans, Angela Royston
(Heinemann Library, 2004)

Index